T0344399

Quick Python 3

Are you a programmer who wants to get started quickly in a new language? This book is for you.

Are you a novice who wants to learn to program? This book is *not* for you.

Are you a Python programmer who needs encyclopaedic information? This book is *not* for you.

Like any mainstream language, Python has loops, if statements, assignment statements, functions, etc. I'll show you what these look like in Python. I won't waste your time telling you what they're good for.

Python has features you may not be familiar with—iterators, list comprehensions, maybe even dictionaries. I'll spend more time on these.

I'll cover some of the library functions I found most immediately useful and tell you where to find more.

In short, this book will help you hit the ground running. Next week, you'll be ready to buy that Python encyclopedia.

Quick Python 3

David Matuszek

CRC Press
Taylor & Francis Group
Boca Raton London New York

CRC Press is an imprint of the
Taylor & Francis Group, an **informa** business

A CHAPMAN & HALL BOOK

First edition published 2023
by CRC Press
6000 Broken Sound Parkway NW, Suite 300, Boca Raton, FL 33487-2742

and by CRC Press
4 Park Square, Milton Park, Abingdon, Oxon, OX14 4RN

CRC Press is an imprint of Taylor & Francis Group, LLC

© 2023 David Matuszek

Library of Congress Cataloging-in-Publication Data
Names: Matuszek, David L., author.
Title: Quick Python 3 / David Matuszek.
Other titles: Quick Python three
Description: First edition. | Boca Raton : CRC Press, 2023. |
Series: Quick programming series | Includes bibliographical references and index.
Identifiers: LCCN 2022036020 (print) | LCCN 2022036021 (ebook) | ISBN 9781032410920 (hbk) | ISBN 9781032410913 (pbk) | ISBN 9781003356219 (ebk)
Subjects: LCSH: Python (Computer program language) | Computer programming.
Classification: LCC QA76.73.P98 M385 2023 (print) | LCC QA76.73.P98 (ebook) |
DDC 005.13/3--dc23/eng/20220930
LC record available at https://lccn.loc.gov/2022036020
LC ebook record available at https://lccn.loc.gov/2022036021

ISBN: 978-1-032-41092-0 (hbk)
ISBN: 978-1-032-41091-3 (pbk)
ISBN: 978-1-003-35621-9 (ebk)

DOI: 10.1201/9781003356219

Typeset in Minion
by MPS Limited, Dehradun

To all my students,
past, present, and future

Contents

Author

I 'M **David Matuszek**, known to most of my students as "Dr. Dave."

I wrote my first program on punched cards in 1963, and immediately got hooked.

I taught my first computer classes in 1970 as a graduate student in computer science at The University of Texas in Austin. I eventually received my PhD from there, and I've been teaching ever since. Admittedly, I spent over a dozen years in industry, but even then I taught as an adjunct for Villanova University.

I finally escaped from industry and joined the Villanova faculty full time for a few years, and then moved to the University of Pennsylvania, where I directed a master's program (MCIT, master's in computer and information technology) for students coming into computer science from another discipline.

Throughout my career, my main interests have been in artificial intelligence (AI) and programming languages. I've used a *lot* of programming languages.

I retired in 2017, but I can't stop teaching, so I'm writing a series of "quick start" books on programming and programming languages. I've also written two science fiction novels, *Ice*

Jockey and *All True Value*, and I expect to write more. Check them out!

And hey, if you're a former student of mine, drop me a note. I'd love to hear from you!

david.matuszek@gmail.com

Preface

THE PURPOSE OF THIS BOOK IS TO GET YOU, a programmer, up and productive in Python as quickly as possible.

Don't buy this book if:

- You aren't already a programmer (in some language), or
- You want a comprehensive guide to Python.

With that out of the way, let's get started.

CHAPTER 1

The Absolute Bare Minimum

1.1 PYTHON AND IDEs

Go to python.org and download the most recent version of Python (it's free). Install it on your computer as you would any other program.

While you're there, you might want to explore the online documentation. A couple of clicks will bring you to docs.python.org/3/, and from there the Library Reference link will bring you to a long list of modules, each containing numerous useful methods.

Included in your Python download you will find a simple ***IDE*** (***Integrated Development Environment***) called IDLE. You have four choices:

- You can spend five minutes learning how to use IDLE. This is what I recommend if you're in a hurry.

- If you are already familiar with a professional IDE such as Eclipse, IntelliJ IDEA, NetBeans, or Jupyter Notebook, there will be a choice of Python plugins you can use. You can spend an indefinite amount of time choosing, downloading, installing, and configuring your new plugin. This is what I recommend after you have gained some familiarity with Python.

- You can run Python from the command line.

- There are several online Python compiler/editors that you can use (search for "Python online"). These are great for just trying a few things out.

1.2 IDLE

When you run IDLE, you get a "Shell" window, into which you can type expressions or statements at the >>> prompt.

- If you type an expression such as 2+2, IDLE will respond with 4 and a new prompt.

- If you enter a statement such as x=2+2, IDLE responds with just a new prompt. (You can see the value assigned by entering the expression x.)

This is a great way to test small amounts of code.

To write complete programs, choose File > New File and enter your code there. You have to save the file before you can run it. The extension .py will be added automatically to the file name, or you can add it yourself. Run your program by choosing Run > Run Module or by hitting F5.

> **Pro tip:** Every time you make a change to your program, you are prompted to save it again before you can run it. You can skip this step by going to Preferences > General and, where it says At Start of Run (F5), choose No Prompt.

Spend a few minutes looking over the menus; there are things in there that can save you time. Notice that the menus differ according to whether you are in a shell window or a file window.

1.3 VARIABLES

Variables do not have a type, and do not have to be declared. Variables come into existence when you assign a value to them.

Example: best_value = 36

> **Convention:** Variable names begin with a lowercase letter or (in special cases) an underscore. For multi-word variable names, most programmers use underscores between words (as above), but some use "camelCase" (sometimes called "studlyCaps") such as bestValue.

> **Caution:** Python's built-in type names and function names are not reserved words, and it is easy to override them accidentally. For example, if you use the name list or abs for a variable, you can no longer use those names to create lists or find absolute values.

1.4 IMPORTANT DATA TYPES

The basic data types are similar to what you're already used to:

- int (*integers*): 73, -15, 12345678901234567890. Integers may be arbitrarily large.

- float (*real numbers*): 3.1416, 6.022e+23.

- bool (logicals, or booleans): True and False. Note that these are capitalized.

- str (*strings*): "Hello World", 'Goodbye'. You can use either single or double quotes. You can insert single quotes inside double-quoted strings, and vice versa. There is no separate "character" type.

- `list` (*array-like lists*): `[1, 2, "Buckle my shoe"]`. Lists aren't exactly arrays, but you can treat them as such. Lists are zero indexed, so if `my_list` holds the above list, `my_list[0]` is 1.

There is also a simple but unusual type:

- `NoneType`, with the single value None. None is an actual value that can be assigned to variables; it is *not* a default value for variables that have not yet been assigned a value. In Python, every function returns a value, and None is most often seen as the result of a function that does not explicitly return a value.

Other data types (*tuples*, *sets*, and *dictionaries*) will be discussed later.

1.5 BASIC ARITHMETIC

- *Add* (+), *subtract* (-), *multiply* (*), and *exponentiation* (**). If both operands are integers, the result is an integer, otherwise the result is a float.

- *Divide* (/). The result of a division using / is always a float.

- *Integer divide* (//). The result of dividing two integers is the integer part of the result, rounded down. If either or both operants of // are floats, the result is a float, rounded down to the nearest integer value. Thus, 10 // 4 is 2, while 10.0 // 4 is 2.0.

- *Modulus* (%). The result of "modding" two integers is the remainder of the division. Thus, 20 % 7 is 6, because 7 goes into 20 twice, with 6 left over. If one or both operands of % are floats, the result is a float. *The % operator has nothing to do with percentages.*

- *Order of precedence*: In a complex expression,

  - Exponentiations are done first, then multiplications and divisions (including modulus), then additions and subtractions.

  - Multiple exponentiations are done right to left; that is, 2**3**4 means 2**(3**4).

  - Other operations of the same precedence are done left to right, so 10-5-2 means (10-5)-2.

  - If in doubt, use parentheses to control the order of operations.

Except in the case of / (which always yields a float), the result of an operation will be an integer if both operands are integer, otherwise it will be a float.

Caution: Languages *do not all agree* what the results should be when using the // or % operators with negative numbers! Avoid this situation or, if you cannot avoid it, experiment until you are sure of the rules in Python. Then add an appropriate comment to your code.

Style: Put spaces around all arithmetic and comparison operators, including the assignment operator (=). This makes your code easier to read.

Conversions between types can be made with the float, int, round, and str functions. For example:

- float(123), float("123"), and float("123.0") all return the floating-point number 123.0.

- round(123.45678, 3) returns the floating point number 123.457, which is rounded to three digits after the decimal point. This is useful for printing numbers more neatly.

- int(56.78) and int("56") both return the integer 56. When converting from a float, the digits after the decimal point are discarded.

- round(56.78) returns 57. The float is rounded to the nearest integer.

- str(*arg*) will return a string version of its argument. Almost anything, not just numbers, can be converted to a string representation.

1.6 COMPARISONS

Comparisons:

- Equals (==), not equal (!=), less than (<), less than or equal (<=), greater than (>), and greater than or equal (>=).

- *Chaining*: Unlike most languages, Python lets you chain comparisons, for example, 2 < 3 < 4 > 2. All comparisons are performed pairwise, and the result is True if every individual comparision is True.

1.7 BOOLEANS

The two *boolean* (logical) values are True and False.

Python has the boolean operators not, and, and or, with the usual meanings. The and and or operators are **short-circuit**; that is, the second operand is evaluated only if necessary.

- In 2 == 2 or f(x), the first part (2 == 2) makes the whole expression True (because True or *anything* is True), so the second part, f(x), is never evaluated.

- Similarly, in 2 == 5 and f(x), the first part (2 == 5) makes the whole expression False, so the second part, f(x), is never evaluated.

The comparison operators (<, <=, ==, !=, >=, >) also work with booleans; True is greater than False.

In a numeric expression, True has the value 1 and False has the value 0. In a boolean expression, all numeric zero values are false, and all nonzero values are true. Using these facts will make your code less explicit.

The special value None indicates "no value," and is treated as false.

An **if expression** results in one of two values, depending on whether the given **condition** is true. The syntax is:

valueIfTrue if *condition* else *valueIfFalse*

1.8 LISTS

A **list** is written as a sequence of values enclosed in square brackets.

A list can be treated as if it were an array. If my_list is a list of 100 values, the first element is my_list[0] and the last element is my_list[99]. You can use the bracket notation both to access a list element and to change its value; for example,

```
my_list[5] = my_list[4] + my_list[3]
```

Conveniently, lists can be accessed from the other end, using negative numbers: my_list[-1] is the same as my_list[99], my_list[-2] is the same as my_list[98], and so on.

The length of a list is given by the function len, so len(my_list) is 100.

1.9 STRINGS

A *string* is written as a sequence of characters enclosed in quote marks. Strings can be concatenated (added together) with the + operator; "Hello" + "World" gives "HelloWorld". You can also leave out the + between literal (quoted) strings and just separate them by spaces or tabs. (Newlines can also be used, if the strings are enclosed in parentheses).

In Python, you can enclose strings in single quotes ('...'), double quotes ("..."), triple single quotes ('''...''') or triple double quotes ("""..."""). You can insert single quotes inside double-quoted strings, double quotes inside single-quoted strings, and either inside triple-quoted strings. Triple-quoted strings may extend across more than one line. Python usually uses single quotes when printing out results.

There is no separate "character" type.

Special characters can be included in strings by "escaping" them (putting a backslash in front of them).

- \n is a "newline" character, however that is encoded on your computer system.

- \t is a tab character. It is a single character, but the amount of space that it represents depends on where tab stops are set in the application used to look at the code.

- \" is a double quote character (useful inside double-quoted strings).

- \' is a single quote character (useful inside single-quoted strings).

- \\ is a backslash character.

- \u*xxxx* or\u*xxxxxxxx* is a Unicode character (four or eight hex digits).

Strings can be indexed as if they were lists. `'HelloWorld'[0]` is `'H'`.

1.10 COMMENTS

Comments begin with a hash mark, #, and continue to the end of the line.

1.11 STATEMENT TYPES

Indentation matters. Statements at the same level must be indented exactly the same amount. Nested statements, for example, statements within a loop body, must be indented relative to the start of the loop. Where Java and the C family of languages use braces, Python uses indentation.

Standard indentation is four spaces. **You may *not* mix spaces with tabs.** However, any IDE and any good text editor can be set to put in four spaces when you hit the Tab key on your keyboard.

The first line of a program may not be indented.

Each statement is written on a line by itself, but if the line contains an unclosed (, [, or {, it may be continued on the next line.

If you want to put two statements on the same line, you can separate them with a semicolon, ;. If you are used to a language in which every statement ends with a semicolon, this will work in Python, it just looks strange to seasoned Python programmers.

If you are using IDLE, it will automatically indent after any line ending with a colon. If it fails to indent, that means you forgot the colon.

Alert. Although I have tried to keep code lines short, some statements may wrap to the next line, especially if you are reading this on a narrow screen. Don't be fooled by this.

Alert. Copying and pasting code from the electronic version of this book may not work. All the code has been tested, but in some cases invisible formatting codes were added to preserve the indentation.

Rather than talk in the abstract about syntax, it's easier to just look at examples of each of the statement types.

1.11.1 Assignment Statements

Assignment statements consist of a *variable*, an *equals sign*, and an *expression*. For example,

```
x = 1
```

Assignment shortcuts use an operator and a single = sign.

- x += y is a shortcut for x = x + y

- x -= y is a shortcut for x = x - y

- ...and so on, for each of the other binary operators.

The "walrus operator," :=, is an assignment operator that can be used within an expression, for example, x = (n := 3 * n) + 1 multiplies the current value of n by 3, assigns the result back into n, then adds 1 to that and puts the result into x. If n is initially 10, the result will be that n is set to 30 and x to 31.

1.11.2 Print "Statements"

Print "statements" are actually calls to a function named print, but everybody uses them as statements. You can give print any number of arguments, and they will all be printed on the same line, with spaces between them.

For example, if x has the value 5, then the function call `print ('x =', x)` will print x = 5.

Each printed line ends with a newline character. If you instead want the following `print` statement to continue on the same line, use `end=""` as the last argument.

`print()` will print a blank line.

1.11.3 If Statements

If statements use the keywords `if` and (optionally) `elif` and `else`.

```
if n == 1:
    print("One")
elif n == 2:
    print("Two")
elif n == 3:
    print("Three")
else:
    print("Many")
    print("or maybe none at all")
```

You can use as many `elif`s as you like, each with an associated condition, and you can have a final `else`. Each `if`, `elif`, or `else` line ends with a colon (:). The statements under the control of each case must be indented.

1.11.4 While Loops

While loops continue to execute as long as the condition is true. For example,

```
n = 5
while n > 0:
    print(n)
    n -= 1
print("Blast off!")
```

The walrus operator can be used in while loops. The above code is equivalent to

```
n = 6
while (n := n - 1) > 0:
    print(n)
print("Blast off!")
```

1.11.5 For Loops

For loops execute their body once for each element of a list, string, tuple, or other iterable type.

```
for i in [5, 4, 3, 2, 1]:
    print(i)
print("Blast off!")
```

or

```
for i in range(5, 0, -1):
    print(i)
print("Blast off!")
```

The range function has three forms:

- range(*b*) will give the numbers 0, 1, 2, etc., up to *but not including b*.

- range(*a*, *b*) will give the numbers *a*, *a*+1, *a*+2, etc., up to *but not including b*.

- range(*a*, *b*, *c*) will give the numbers *a*, *a*+*c*, *a*+*c*+*c*, *a*+*c*+*c*+*c*, etc., up to (or down to) *but not including b*.

Technical note: The value returned by range is not a list, but rather an iterator (more on those later). If you need a list, use list(range(...)).

1.11.6 Import Statements

Python has some functions already "built in." For example, abs(n) will give you the absolute value of the number n. If x is a list, len(x) will return the length of the list; or if x is a string, len(x) will return the number of characters in the string.

Many more functions are available but are not built in; you have to *import* them from a module. (A "module" is just a file containing code.) For example, the square root and natural logarithm functions, sqrt and log, can be imported from the math module.

```
from math import sqrt, log
```

Now if you want the square root of a number x, just say sqrt(x).

For small programs, it is easy to import everything at once from a module. For example,

```
from math import *
```

This form of import statement is not recommended for larger programs. In addition to being less explicit, there is the risk of inadvertently importing the same name (with different meanings) from different modules.

The standard Python distribution comes with about 300 modules; many more are available, both commercial and free; several of these are described in the appendices. Before writing code to solve problems in a given domain, it is a good idea to first check to see what is already available.

1.12 INPUT FROM THE USER

To ask the user for input, you can call the function input (*prompt*). For example,

```python
name = input("What is your name? ")
print("Hello,", name)
```

You can omit the prompt, in which case the user will be left staring at a blank screen and wondering why the program isn't doing anything.

The result of a call to input is always a string. If you are expecting an integer or a float, you can use the int or float functions to convert the string to the desired type. For example,

```python
question = "How old are you, " + name + "? "
age = int(input(question))
```

If the user types in something that can't be made into an integer, an error will result. We'll deal with error handling later.

1.13 FUNCTIONS

To define a function, use the word def, the name of the function, a parenthesized list of parameters, and a colon. Follow this with the indented body of the function. When you have a value to return, put the value in a return statement. For example:

```python
def largest(a, b, c):
    """Return the largest of a, b, and c."""
    if a >= b and a >= c:
        return a
    elif b >= a and b >= c:
        return b
    return c
```

(We could have put the final `return` statement into an `else` part, but there's no need to. It will be executed if the `if-elif` statement doesn't do anything.)

The second line of the function is a ***docstring***, used to document the purpose of the function. By convention, triple-quoted strings are used, even if the string is only a single line. If the docstring is more than one line, all lines should be indented the same amount, and the closing triple quote should be on a line by itself.

Docstrings should be written as full sentences. The first sentence (ending in a period) is considered to be a summary line. Documenting each function in this way is optional but strongly recommended. For any function with a docstring, the function `help(`***function_name***`)` will print that string.

Every function returns a value. If you don't specify a return value, the function will return None. (This is an actual legal value, of type `NoneType`, so you can assign it to a variable, or ask if a variable is equal to it.)

A function may be defined within another function, and is then local to the containing function.

1.14 SYNTAX

There are no new concepts in what we've covered so far; it's all just syntax. Syntax is boring. How do you learn boring material?

Practice.

Pick some simple program to write, and write it. For example, make change for any amount (in dollars, quarters, dimes, nickels, and pennies). Determine whether an input number is prime or composite. Find the average of numbers in a list. Whatever.

Of course, this is optional. After all, if you can learn to ride a bicycle by reading a book about it, you can learn Python without programming in it.

1.15 ORDER OF EXECUTION

Not everything in a Python program has to be within a function; you can (and usually will) have some "top-level" statements. Very short programs may consist entirely of top-level statements, with no function definitions.

Python programs are evaluated from beginning (first line) to end (last line). Top level-statements will be evaluated as they occur. Evaluating a function definition (def) causes the function to be defined, but it won't be executed until some other statement calls it.

Functions are defined dynamically, that is, when a def is evaluated, and must be defined before they can be called. As in most languages, there is no restriction on the **lexical ordering** of functions (the order in which they appear in a listing).

It is common for a program to consist of a collection of functions, with the last line of the program being a single top-level call to a "main" function. Often this "main" function is named main, but not always.

1.16 SUMMARY

You should now be able to understand everything about the following program.

```
# Program to print prime numbers

def is_prime(n):
    """Test if a number n is prime."""
    divisor = 2
    while divisor * divisor <= n:
```

```
        if n % divisor == 0:
            return False
        divisor += 1
    return True

def print_primes(limit):
    for i in range(2, limit + 1):
        if is_prime(i):
            print(i, end=' ')

n = input("Print all primes up to: ")
print_primes(int(n))
```

If the is_prime function is called with 1, it will report True, indicating that 1 is a prime number (it is not). Can you correct this problem?

What will is_prime do if given a negative number?

1.17 WAIT, THAT'S IT?

Congratulations! If you've made it this far (and tried some of the things out on your computer), you now know enough to write some pretty complicated programs. Seriously.

Of course, if you stop here, any Python programs you write *will* be complicated. Python has more data types, statement types, and functions that will make your life easier and your programs simpler. This section has been titled "The Absolute Bare Minimum" for a reason.

Keep reading!

CHAPTER 2

Better Tools

2.1 OBJECT NOTATION

Lists and strings (which you have seen), and sets and dictionaries (which are coming up soon) are **objects**. There is a special terminology for talking about objects:

- A **method** is a function defined on an object.

- You don't "call" methods, you *send messages to an object*. This is unwieldy, so I like to say you *talk to* objects.

Along with this, there is a special notation for using objects:

1. Name the object you are talking to.

2. Put a period (.).

3. Write the method name, along with any arguments (comma separated and in parentheses).

For example, if s is the string "Hello World", then s.lower() is the string "hello world". You can think of this as saying, "Hey s, give me a lowercase version of yourself."

DOI: 10.1201/9781003356219-2

2.2 LISTS

A Python *list* is an indexable sequence of values, not necessarily all of the same type. The first index is 0. You can create a list by writing a comma-separated sequence of values enclosed in brackets, [].

Examples:

- s = ["Mary", 23, "A+"]

- name = s[0] # name is now "Mary"

- s[1] += 1 # s is now ["Mary", 24, "A+"]

- The empty list is written as [].

You can create a list of an arbitrary size by "multiplying" it by an integer. The integer must be to the right of the * operator.

- [0] * 4 # result is [0, 0, 0, 0]

- [None] * 100 # result is 100 None's

- [2, 4] * 3 # result is [2, 4, 2, 4, 2, 4]

If *x* is a list, and you say *y* = *x*, then *y* becomes *another name for the same list*, not a copy of *x*. That is, any change you make to *y* also changes *x*, and vice versa.

Here are two useful *functions* on lists:

- len(*my_list*) returns the number of elements in the list.

- sorted(*my_list*) returns a copy of the list with the elements in ascending order.

Here are two useful *methods* on lists:

- *my_list*.append(*value*) adds *value* to the end of *my_list* and returns None.

- *my_list*.pop() removes the last element of *my_list* and returns it.

- *my_list*.sort() sorts the list and returns None.

You can take "slices" of a list, giving you a new list containing some of the elements of the original list. If *my_list* is a list and *i* and *j* are integers, then

- *my_list*[*i*:*j*] is a copy of the elements from *my_list*[*i*] up to but not including my_list[*j*].

- *my_list*[*i*:] is a copy of the elements starting at *my_list*[*i*] and continuing to the end.

- *my_list*[:*j*] is a copy of the elements starting at *my_list*[0] up to but not including *my_list*[*j*].

- *my_list*[:] is a copy of the entire list.

Negative numbers can be used as indices, with -1 indicating the last element of the list. A step size can be included, as *my_list* [*i*:*j*:*step*], and the *step* may also be negative.

You can also use slice notation on the left-hand side of an assignment operator. If you assign a list of values to a slice, those values replace the values in the slice. The list of values does not have to be the same length as the slice it replaces. For example, if x = [0, 1, 2, 3] and you assign x[1:3] = [11, 22, 33], the result will be that x gets the value [0, 11, 22, 33, 3].

> **Pro tip:** You can treat a string as a list of letters, for example, `"abcdef"[2:5]` is `"cde"`.

Since any value can be put in a list, you can make a list of lists, for example, `grades = [["Mary", "A+"], ["Donald", "C-"]]`. To get individual elements, you have to index the outer and the inner lists separately: `grades[1]` is `["Donald", "C-"]`, so `grades[1][0]` is `"Donald"`.

> **Caution:** *Do not* attempt to make a list of lists by using a construction such as `[[None] * 3] * 2`. It will appear to work, but in fact every value in the outer list will be a reference to the same inner list.

You can create a "two-dimensional" list with code like this:

```
x = [0] * 3
for i in range(0, 3):
    x[i] = [0] * 5
```

The initial assignment creates an array of zeros, then the loop replaces each zero with an array of zeros.

2.3 TUPLES

A *tuple* consists of zero or more values separated by commas and enclosed in parentheses; for example, `("John", 23)`. When a tuple is by itself on the left or right side of an assignment, the parentheses may be omitted, for example,

```
a, b, c = 1, 2, 3
```

> **Technical note:** A zero-tuple is written as `()`, while a one-tuple is written by putting a comma after the single value, like this: `(3,)`. These forms probably aren't very useful in general.

Tuples are useful for keeping a small number of values together as a single unit. For example, you might want to write a function that returns the x-y coordinates of an object, or the largest and smallest values in a list.

The built-in function divmod returns a tuple. Seven goes into 20 twice, with six left over (20 // 7 == 2 and 20 % 7 == 6). If you want both these values, you can use divmod(20, 7), which returns the tuple (2, 6).

Here are some of the things you can do with tuples:

- x = (1, 2, 3) # x now holds the tuple (1, 2, 3)

- x = 1, 2, 3 # same as above

- a, b, c = x # a is now 1, b is 2, and c is 3

- a, b, c = "xyz" # a is now "x", b is "y", and c is "z"

- y = x[1] # y is now 2 (tuples are zero-indexed)

- z = x[1:] # ok to use slices; z is now (2, 3)

- a, b = b, a # the values of a and b are interchanged

Tuples are **immutable**: You cannot change their contents. For example, if x is (1, 2, 3), then x[0] = 5 is illegal.

2.4 SETS

A set is a collection of values, not necessarily all the same type. A set literal is written as braces around a comma-separated list. For example:

```
s = {10, "ten", "X"}
```

The empty set (the one with no elements) cannot be written as {}, because that's an empty dictionary (see the next section). Use set() instead.

Sets have two important properties:

- Sets have no duplicate elements. A value is either *in* the set, or it is *not in* the set. In fact, in and not in are operators, so you could ask 10 in s (which is True) or "TEN" not in s (also True).

- The order of elements in a set is unspecified, so you cannot index into a set.

You can use a for loop to go through each element of the set in turn, as long as you don't care in what order the elements are processed.

```
for elem in s:
    print(elem)
```

If the order of elements is important, use a list rather than a set. To convert between lists and sets, use the list and set functions.

If you are familiar with sets from mathematics, Python provides the most common operations: union, intersection, difference, and set difference. These can be written either as operators or as method calls.

- *set1* | *set2* or *set1*.union(*set2*) returns the set of elements that are in either *set1* or *set2*, or both.

- *set1* & *set2* or *set1*.intersection(*set2*) returns the set of elements that are in both *set1* and *set2*.

- *set1* - *set2* or *set1*.difference(*set2*) returns the set of elements that are in *set1* but not in *set2*.

- *set1* ^ *set2* or *set1*.symmetric_difference(*set2*) returns the set of elements that are in exactly one of the sets.

- *set1*.issubset(*set2*) returns True if every element of *set1* is also in *set2*.

- *set1*.issuperset(*set2*) returns True if every element of *set2* is also in *set1*.

The comparison operators (<, <=, ==, !=, >=, >) can also be used to test subset/superset and equality/inequality relationships between two sets. *set1* < *set2* is True if *set1* is a *proper* subset of *set2*, that is, *set1* is a subset of *set2* but not equal to it.

Elements can also be added to a set or removed from a set.

- *set*.add(*element*) adds *element* to *set*. If *element* is already in *set,* this does nothing.

- *set*.discard(*element*) removes *element* from *set* if it is present. If *element* isn't in *set*, this does nothing.

- *set*.remove(*element*) removes *element* from *set*, or raises a KeyError if *element* isn't in *set*.

- *set*.pop() removes and returns an *arbitrary element* from *set*, or raises a KeyError if *set* is empty. Your code should not depend on some particular element being returned.

- *set*.clear() removes all elements from *set*.

2.5 DICTIONARIES

A *dictionary* (of type dict) provides a fast way of looking something up. A dictionary literal is written as zero or more *key*: *value* pairs enclosed in braces, { }. For example, you might define a "phone book" dictionary as follows:

```
phones = {"Alice":5551212, "Jill":5556789, "Bob":5559999}
```

Keys must be unique; you can have only one value associated with a key. Values do not have to be unique; many keys may have the same value.

Once you have a dictionary, there are three ways of looking something up in it. Pay special attention to where parentheses ( ) are used and where brackets [ ] are used.

- `phones["Jill"]` will return 5556789. If the key is not found, for example if you try `phones["Xavier"]`, a KeyError will result.

- `phones.get(`*key*`)` works like `phones[`*key*`]`, except that if the key is not found, the value None is returned.

- `phones.get(`*key*`, `*default_value*`)` returns the value associated with *key,* or the *default_value* if there is no such key.

You can add something to the dictionary by assignment:

```
phones["Xavier"] = 5556666
```

This also works for changing the value associated with the key. For example, you could update someone's phone number this way.

There is a special command, del, for removing something from a dictionary:

```
del phones["Xavier"]
```

The del command will give a KeyError if the key is not in the dictionary, so check before using del. (You can use the in and not in set operators to test if a key is in the dictionary.)

As with sets, the elements of a dictionary are stored in whatever order Python thinks best. It may vary from one implementation to another.

Not everything can be used as a key. Keys must be *immutable*. That's a long discussion in itself, but the short form is this: strings, numbers, tuples, and booleans make good keys. Any object for which the components may change (such as lists, sets, and dictionaries) may *not* be used as keys.

2.6 STRING METHODS

Most of the things you can do with strings are methods, not functions. That is, they have the form *string.method (arguments)*.

There are a lot of string methods. Many of the most useful are listed in Appendix A. Here, we discuss only a couple of the most useful and/or confusing string methods.

- *string1*.split(*string2*) returns a list of the substrings of *string1* that are separated by *string2*. If the *string2* argument is omitted, whitespace is used as the separator. This saves typing when you want a list of strings. For example, 'one two three'.split()returns the list ['one', 'two', 'three'].

- *string*.join(*list_of_strings*) returns a single string, with the elements of the *list_of_strings* separated by *string*. For example, '<='.join(['a', 'b', 'ab']) returns the string 'a<=b<=ab'. This can be confusing to read because *string* is most often either a single blank, ' ', or an empty string, ''.

A formatted string, or *f-string*, is prefixed with f or F. In an f-string, *any expression* surrounded by braces, {}, is replaced by its value. For example, the string `'pi is {round(pi, 4)}.'` results in `'pi is 3.1416.'`.

To put a brace character in an f-string, double it.

2.7 LOOPS FOR OBJECTS

Iterables, such as lists, tuples, sets, and dictionaries can be iterated over with for loops.

2.7.1 Looping over Lists

If you want to do something with every element of a list or other iterable type, you can use a for loop. A simple for loop looks like this:

```
for e in my_list:
    print(e)
```

If you need to work with not only the elements in the list, but also their position in the list, you can use a more complicated version of the for loop:

```
for i in range(0, len(my_list)):
    print(my_list[i], "is at", i)
```

The enumerate function provides a better way to get (**index**, **value**) tuples. The above code can be replaced with

```
for index, value in enumerate(my_list):
    print(value, "is at", index)
```

Note that parentheses around the returned tuples are optional.

Simpler is generally better, so don't use a loop that gets indices unless you really need them.

2.7.2 Looping over Sets

The simple form of the `for` loop works for sets:

```
for e in my_set:
    print(e)
```

The `enumerate` method also works for sets. However, it is worth repeating that sets cannot be subscripted and should always be treated as having no definite order.

2.7.3 Looping over Dictionaries

The simple loop also works for dictionaries, but in this case, what is assigned to the loop variable is just the key, not the entire *key*: *value* pair:

```
for k in my_dict:
    print(k) # prints just the keys
```

To make this more explicit, you could use the keys method of a dictionary:

```
for k in my_dict.keys():
    print(k) # prints just the keys
```

You can also just print the values by using the `values` method:

```
for v in my_dict.values():
    print(v) # prints just the values
```

You can print both keys and values by looping over just the keys and, for each key, looking up the value:

```
for k in my_dict:
    print(k, "->", my_dict[k])
```

Dictionaries have an additional method, items. This method *appears* to return a list of (***key***, ***value***) tuples:

```
for t in my_dict.items():
    print(t) # prints (key, value) tuples
```

In reality, what items returns is not a list, but is a ***dynamic view*** of the dictionary items. Each item returned is in fact a (***key***, ***value***) tuple, but if you change the contents of the dictionary while looping through it, you could get some unexpected and unwelcome results.

Tuples can be unpacked directly in the for loop. The parentheses around the tuple may be omitted.

```
for k, v in my_dict.items():
    print(k, "is", v)
```

2.8 HANDING EXCEPTIONS

Errors happen. A program may try to divide a number by zero, or send a message to None, or read in a file that isn't there. When this happens, Python will ***raise an exception***.

Every exception type has a name. In Python, there is almost no distinction between an "error" and an "exception." Either, if not handled, will cause the program to terminate.

If you know where an error is likely to occur, you can deal with it. For example, you might use the input function to ask the user for an integer. Whatever the user types will be returned as a string, which you can convert to an integer by using the int function—unless the user types in something other than digits, in which case you will get a ValueError.

To handle this problem, you can use the try-except or
try-except-finally statement. It has this general form:

```
try:
    # code that could go wrong
except SomeErrorType:
    # what to do if it goes wrong
finally:
    # what to do afterwards
```

The finally part is optional. If present, it will be executed
whether or not the error occurs.

Here's an example:

```
number = None
while number is None:
try:
    n = input("Enter an integer: ")
    number = int(n)
except Exception:
    print("Try again!")
print("Your number is", number)
```

In detail, here's how the above example works:

- The variable number is set to None.

- Upon entering the while loop, number equals None, so the
  body of the loop is executed.

- The input function waits for the user to enter something,
  then stores it (as a string) in n.

- The int function tries to convert the string n into a
  number.

- If `int` succeeds,

  - The result is put into `number`, the except part is skipped, and control returns to the top of the loop,

  - Since `number` is no longer equal to `None`, the loop exits.

- If `int` fails,

  - `int` raises an exception,

  - Control goes to the except part, skipping over any statements that may remain in the `try` part,

  - `"Try again!"` is printed out, and control returns to the top of the loop,

  - Since `number` is still equal to `None`, the loop body is executed again.

- When the user enters a valid integer, the loop exits and prints out the number the user entered.

Here are some important points to remember:

- If an error occurs anywhere between `try` and `except`, control goes *immediately* to the except part. Any remaining code in the `try` part will not be executed.

- The code in a `finally` part will *always* be executed. If code in the `try` or except part executes a `return` statement, the code in `finally` will be executed before the function returns.

If an error occurs in a function, but the error is not within a `try`-`except` statement, then the exception is passed up to the calling location. If that location is within a `try`-`except` statement, the exception is handled there, otherwise that function will also immediately return to its calling location. In this way, each function carries the exception to its calling location, all the way up the call sequence, until one of them catches the exception. If the exception is never caught, the program terminates with an error.

Python defines a *large* number of exception types, so that you can do something different for each exception type. For simple programs you can just use the catch-all type Exception, but this is not recommended for larger programs.

Usually, the hard part of handling errors is figuring out what to do when they occur.

2.9 TYPE CONVERSIONS

When called as a function, a type *name* serves as a constructor. Given an argument of a different type, the function will (when possible) return a value of the named type. For example:

- int(5.7) # returns 5

- int("5") # returns 5

- float(5) # returns 5.0

- float("5.7") # returns 5.7

- bool("False") # returns True

  - The following things are considered false: False, None, 0, 0.0, empty strings, empty lists, empty sets, empty tuples, and empty dictionaries.

- str([1, 2, 3]) # result is '[1, 2, 3]'

Other data types that can be used as conversion functions are list, set, tuple, and dict (dictionary).

- When you convert from a dict to any of the other types, you get only the keys, not the values.

- You can convert a list, set, or tuple to a dict only if the elements are grouped in twos, for example, a list of 2-tuples (tuples with two elements).

- Sets have no intrinsic ordering, so converting to or from a set does not necessarily preserve the order of the elements.

The function type(x) will return a value that can be compared to the *name* of a type (*not* to a string representation of that name). For example, the test type(5) == int will return True, but type(5) == "int" will return False.

The function isinstance (*value, type*) tests whether *value* is of the named *type*. To test whether the value is one of a number of simple types, the type may be a tuple of those types, (*type1, type2, ...*), or a *type union, type1 | type2 | ...*, in which case isinstance tests whether *value* is of any of the named types in the tuple. However, instanceof cannot test for a *genericized type* such as list[int].

2.10 SCOPE

The scope of a name is the part of the program in which the name has meaning and can be used. Python's scope rules are unusual; they follow an "LEGB rule": Local, Enclosed, Global, Built-in. To understand this rule, it helps to remember that (1) variables are defined by being assigned a value and (2) functions/methods may be nested within other functions/methods.

- Variables may be declared to be global or nonlocal by a statement of the form global *var1, ..., varN* or nonlocal *var1, ..., varN*. The declaration must precede any use of the variable.

- **Local**: A variable is local to a function if it is a parameter, or if it is assigned a value within that function and not explicitly declared to be global or nonlocal.

- **Enclosed**: A variable in a function can refer to a variable declared in an enclosing function, provided either (1) the variable is not assigned a value in this function or (2) it is declared in a `nonlocal` statement.

- **Global**: A variable declared at the top level (not in a function or method) is global, and can be referenced throughout the program. A variable in a function can refer to a global variable, provided either (1) the variable is not assigned a value in this function or in an enclosing function or (2) it is declared in a `global` statement.

- **Built-in**: A variable not declared otherwise in the program might be a built-in variable. Some examples are `list`, `print`, and `divmod`.

When a variable is nonlocal (enclosed) or global, it is good documentation to declare it as such, even when the variable is not assigned a value within the function.

Global variables are generally regarded as undesirable and should be avoided wherever possible. Functions that use global variables are:

- no longer self-contained, and can be understood and debugged only in context;

- harder to test because the test must include code to set the globals properly; and

- harder to reuse in another project because they are context-dependent.

Globals can be avoided by adding extra parameters to functions, and by adding instance variables to classes.

Some programmers use the convention of starting the name of every global variable with an underscore. This convention does not affect the actual scope of the variable.

2.11 FILE I/O

To read or write a file, you must do three things: (1) open the file, (2) use the file, and (3) close the file.

- with open (*file_name, mode*) as *file*: *statements* will open the file, execute the *statements* once, then close the file. This is the easiest and safest way to process a file.

  - The *mode* is one of:

    - 'r' to read the file (this is the default if *mode* is omitted).

    - 'w' to erase and write the file.

    - 'a' to append to the end of an existing file.

    - 'r+' to both read and write.

    - 'rb', 'wb', 'ab', 'rb+' to do binary input/output.

  - Since the *statements* part is executed only once, it typically consists of a loop that processes each line in turn.

  - Indentation is as usual: the *statements* are indented under the with line.

- *file* = open(*file_name, mode*) opens and returns (in variable *file*) a reference to the named file; mode is a described for with open.

- *file*.read() will read in and return the entire file as a single string, including any newline characters.

- *file*.readline() reads and returns a line of text, including the terminating newline (if any). If the empty string is returned, the end of the file has been reached.

- *file*.readlines() reads the entire file and returns it as a list of strings, including terminating newlines.

- Input files may be iterated over: for line in file: *statements* will read each line in the file, assign it to the variable *line*, and execute the *statements*. The *statements* are indented as usual.

- *file*.write (*string*) writes the string to the file, and returns the number of characters written.

- *file*.close() closes the file. **Mandatory.** Leaving the file open when you are done with it is likely to cause problems.

As an example, here is some code to count the number of lines in a text file.

```
count = 0
with open(file_name, 'r') as f:
    while f.readline():
        count += 1
```

For historical reasons, the character or characters used to denote a "newline" ('\n') are not the same on Windows files, old Macintosh files, and Mac OS X/Linux files. Reading or writing text files (non-binary files) will automatically convert platform-specific line endings to the current platform. **Reading or writing binary files as if they were text files will corrupt them.** Text files, on the other hand, can be read and written as binary without harm.

2.12 PICKLING

Serializing (sometimes called *marshalling*) an object is turning it into a linear stream of bytes. This can be done to save an object on a file, or to transmit it to another process. The byte stream can be *deserialized* (*unmarshalled*) to reconstruct the original object.

The most common way to serialize Python objects is called *pickling*. Python can also use JSON and XML for serialization, but these do not support as many object types.

Python values and most built-in objects can be pickled, including user-defined classes and functions at the top level of a module. Recursive and interconnected objects can be pickled. Generators, lambda functions, database connections, and threads are a few things that cannot be pickled.

To pickle or unpickle objects, first `import pickle`, then use the following methods:

- `pickle.dump` (*object, file*) — Saves *object* onto the *file*, which must have been opened in `'wb'` (write binary) mode.

- *variable* = `pickle.load` (*file*) — Reconstructs the object previously written to *file*, which must have been opened in `'rb'` (read binary) mode.

- *str* = `pickle.dumps` (*object*) — Saves *object* into the variable *str* as a string.

- *object* = `pickle.loads` (*str*) — Reconstructs the object previously written to the string *str*.

Pickling is **not secure**. A pickle file can contain code objects and data to attack your system. Make sure that anything you unpickle comes from a trusted source and has not been tampered with in transit.

CHAPTER 3

Classes

A CLASS DEFINES A NEW *type*, along with a **constructor** for making values of that type. Values of that type are **objects**, and each such **object** will contain the variables and methods described in the class.

Here is an analogy: A *class* is like a cake recipe, while *objects* are the cakes you can make by following the recipe. The variables in the Cake class might include sugar, flour, and butter, while the methods might include mix, bake, and serve.

3.1 CLASSES AND INHERITANCE

The syntax for defining a class is

class *ClassName* (*superclass*):
    variable and method definitions

Classes are arranged in a **hierarchy**, with the object class at the top. Every class (except object itself) has a **superclass**, and it **inherits** variables and methods from that superclass. That is, all

DOI: 10.1201/9781003356219-3

variables and methods defined in (or inherited by) the superclass are available to the new class.

For example, you might define a class Person with variables name and age and a method greet. Every object of this type will have its own copies of those variables, and its own reference to the greet method. If you then create a class Customer as a subclass of Person, every object of type Customer will have its own name and age variables and a greet method, plus whatever additional variables and methods you declare in Customer(for example, a list of purchases).

The special class object is the "root" of all classes. If you omit *superclass* when you define a class, it defaults to having the superclass object. Every class inherits from object, either directly or indirectly.

> **Terminology:** As a noun, "instance" means the same as "object." However, we usually use "instance" when talking about a particular object (john is an instance of Person), or when we are using the word as an adjective (name is an instance variable of the class Person).

> **Terminology:** "Field" and "attribute" are other names for "instance variable."

Example (very bad) class definition:

```python
class Person(object):
    name = 'Joe'
    age = 23

    def say_hi(self):
        print('Hello, Joe.')
```

- To create an instance (object) of a class, use the name of the class as if it were a function name, for example, p = Person(). Used in this way, the class name acts as a ***constructor***; it constructs a new object.

- We can access the fields of object p using ***dot notation:*** p.name is 'Joe' and p.age is 23.

- We can modify the fields of p, for example by saying p.name = 'Jack'.

- We can use dot notation to "talk to" the object p, or more formally, "send a message to" the object p: p.say_hi() tells p to say_hi, and p will respond by printing Hello, Joe..

  Convention: Class names always begin with a capital letter, and variable and function names always begin with a lower-case letter.

Unfortunately, every newly created instance of this class will be exactly the same. We would like to create instances of Person with different inital values for name and age. To do this, we have to explore a special variable: self.

3.2 CONSTRUCTORS AND SELF

If you are familiar with classes and objects in some other language, then classes and objects are very similar in Python—except you may have trouble with the word self, which seems to be required everywhere.

Remember that each object we create from a class has its own copy of each of the fields (instance variables) of that class. If we have two Person objects named joe and jane, then each of them will have a name field and an age field.

Briefly, the name self used inside a class definition is the particular object we are talking to.

Every method within a class must have `self` **as its first parameter.**

Here's a better class definition:

```python
class Person(object):

    def __init__(self, name, age):
        self.name = name
        self.age = age

    def say_hi(self):
        print('Hello', self.name)
```

When you construct an object, you probably want to specify the values of its instance variables. For example, each `Person` object should be created with its own `name` and its own `age`. This is done by including a special method named `__init__` in the class definition. (That's `init` with two underscores before and two after.) `__init__` is an *initializer*—it is called *automatically from the constructor* when you construct a new object.

> **Technical note:** Python has a number of *dunder methods*, which begin and end with double underscores. Dunder methods are used internally, and seldom called directly.

To create an object, use the name of the class as if it were a function name, and supply values for all the parameters *except* `self`. Inside the `__init__` method, use the form `self.` *variable* = *value*   to initialize instance variables.

In the above example, we would create an object `jill` by saying `jill = Person('Jill', 30)`. Inside the initializer `__init__`, a `name` instance variable is created by assigning a value to `self.name`, and an `age` instance variable is created by assigning a value to `self.age`.

Outside the class definition, we "talk to" an object by using dot notation, for example, jill.age or jill.say_hi(). But *inside* the class definition, the object is talking to "itself," so we say self.age and self.say_hi().

So, what is self? It is an *explicit* first parameter of every method, and a *prefix* argument of every message we send to an object. In the definition of say_hi, self must be given as the first parameter; when we say jill.say_hi(), jill is the argument passed to the method as the value of self (see Figure 3.1).

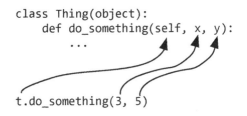

FIGURE 3.1   The word self as a prefix argument.

If a method refers to an instance variable in the same class, the word self must be used. If one method of a class calls another method of the same class, the word self must be used. Any variables (or methods) not tagged with the name self are just local to the method they are in.

```
def get_older(self):
    self.age += 1

def get_much_older(self, years):
    for i in range(0, years):
        self.get_older()
```

Technical note: self is just a parameter name, so in theory you could replace it with any other name. This would be strongly against convention.

Unlike some other object-oriented languages, an object does not have a fixed and unvarying set of instance variables. You can add an instance variable to an object simply by assignment; for example, you could say jill.occupation = 'scientist'. This affects only jill; other Person objects are unchanged. Similarly, you can use the del operation to remove an instance variable from a particular object.

> **Important debugging note:** When defining and using classes and objects, the most common error is supplying *too many arguments* or *not enough arguments*. This is almost always the result of forgetting to use self somewhere.

> **Comparison with Java:** Java's this is equivalent to the Python's self, with two differences: (1) this is a keyword, but self is a variable name; and (2) this is usually implicit, but self must be explicitly used every time.

3.3 SUBCLASSES

A class inherits all the instance variables and methods of its superclass. (It is a *subclass* of its superclass.) For example, you might define a Friend class as a subclass of Person.

```
class Friend(Person):
    def smile(self):
        print('¯\_(^-^)_/¯')

meg = Person('Margaret', 25)
bob = Friend('Robert', 33)
```

When you create meg as an instance of Person, meg will have the say_hi, get_older, and get_much_older methods and the __init__ initializer, but not the smile method. When you create bob as a Friend, bob will have all these things, and will also have a smile method.

You can *override* (replace) any inherited method by providing another method with the same name, for example,

```
def say_hi(self, extra):
    print('Hi!', extra)
```

If you override a method in a subclass, you can still access the overridden method by using super() as a prefix. For example,

```
def say_hi(self, extra):
    super().say_hi()
    print(extra)
```

You usually write a subclass when you want everything in its superclass, but you want the subclass to have additional information in it. For example, a Friend object is a Person, so it should have a name and an age, but maybe you also want it to have a nickname. In this case you will need to write a new __init__ method, overrriding the inherited one.

In the initializer for Friend you *could* copy and paste all the work done in the initializer for Person, but it is much better style to just call that initializer. In this case you *do* call __init__ directly. For example, the Friend initializer might look like this:

```
def __init__(self, name, age, nick):
    super().__init__(name, age)
    self.nickname = nick
```

If you write a subclass because you want only some of the things in its superclass, but not all of them, this is an indication that your classes would benefit from being reorganized.

3.4 PRINTING OBJECTS

The print method takes any number of arguments, converts each argument into a string by calling its __str__ method, and prints them. (As with __init__, that's two underscores before and after the name.)

All classes have a __str__ method inherited from object. It is a good idea to override this method. If you don't, your objects will be printed something like this:

```
<__main__.Friend object at 0x1064728d0>
```

In the case of a Friend object, your method might look something like this:

```
def __str__(self):
    return self.name + "'s age is " + str(self.age)
```

and print(meg) would result in:

```
Margaret's age is 19
```

In the above, Margret's age is an integer, and we can't add an integer to a string, so we had to explicitly convert her age to a string by calling the function str(self.age). Once you've defined the method __str__ in your class, you can call the function str on objects of that class, for example by saying str(meg).

Similar to str(x), the repr(x) function returns a string representing the object x, as defined by its __repr__(self) method. The difference is that str is used by the print method and should provide a humanly readable string, whereas the repr method is used during debugging and development, and should be detailed and unambiguous.

__str__ and __repl__ are inherited "dunder" methods which you can override with your own versions, then call indirectly with str(x) and repl(x).

3.5 COMPARING OBJECTS

The equality (==) and inequality (!=) operators work well for Python's built-in object types. When you define your own classes, however, == will return False when comparing two distinct objects (but see below).

It is important to keep in mind the distinction between *equal* and *identical.*

- Two objects *a* and *b* are ***equal*** if every part of *a* is the same as the corresponding part of *b*; if you change *a*, *b* might or might not change. Testing for equality requires testing all the parts.

- If *a* and *b* are ***identical***, then they are just two different names for the same object; changing that object by doing something to *a* means that *b* also sees the change. Testing for identity just involves testing whether *a* and *b* both refer to the same location in memory.

- Assignment, *a* = *b*, never makes a copy of an object *b*; it just makes *a* refer to the same object as *b*.

- When you use an object as an argument to a function, the function gets a reference to the original object, not a copy.

- *a* is *b* tests whether *a* and *b* refer to the same object; *a* is not *b* tests whether they are different (but possibly equal) objects.

For your own class, you can define equality and ordering by defining some special methods in the class. (All these names use double underscores.)

- __eq__(self, *other*) should return True if you consider the objects self and *other* to be equal, and False otherwise. Identical objects should be considered to be equal (you can test identity with the is operator). This method will be called when your objects are compared using ==.

- __ne__(self, *other*) will be called when objects are compared using !=.

- __lt__(self, *other*) will be called when objects are compared using <.

- __le__(self, *other*) will be called when objects are compared using <=.

- __ge__(self, *other*) will be called when objects are compared using >=.

- __gt__(self, *other*) will be called when objects are compared using >.

These methods are all independent. Defining some of them does *not* automatically define others. For example, if you define an __eq__ method, __ne__ does not magically pop into being. If you define one of these methods, you should define all six.

We usually think of the comparison operators as comparing sizes, or magnitudes; but if you define your own comparison operators, you can use them for any kind of ordering you like. This has already been done for strings; the operators use lexicographical (alphabetical) ordering, with all capital letters less than all lowercase letters.

3.6 BINDINGS

In a technical sense, every value in Python is an object. However, some objects are *immutable*: They cannot be changed. For example, the number 5 is immutable; you cannot change a 5 to a 6. If you have a variable x whose value is 5 (we say x is *bound* to 5), you can use an assignment statement to change the binding of x to 6, but 5 is still 5.

When you do an assignment, you **bind** the variable to a value. If you then assign that variable to a new variable, the binding is simply copied.

```
a = 5 # bind a to 5
b = a # copy a's binding into b
a = 6 # change the binding of a
print(b) # b is still bound to 5
```

Numbers, strings, booleans, and tuples are immutable. A list, however, is **mutable**: You can change the values in a list, but it's still the same list. Sets, dictionaries, and most other objects are mutable.

Binding works the same way for mutable objects as it does for immutable objects.

```
a = [1, 2, 3] # bind a to the list
b = a # copy a's binding into b
a = [4, 5, 6] # change the binding of a
print(b) # b is still bound to [1, 2, 3]
```

Changing the values in a mutable object *does not change* any variable bindings.

```
a = [1, 2, 3] # bind a to the list
b = a # copy a's binding into b
a[0] = 99 # change the list, not the bindings
print(b) # b still bound to the same list,
    # but the list is now [99, 2, 3]
```

When a function is called, the values of the arguments in the call are bound to the parameters of the function; in other words, those values are assigned to the parameters. When a function returns, it does *not* copy the parameter values back into the argument list, but any mutable objects passed to the function could have been changed in the function.

```
def foo(a, b):
    a[0] = 99
    b = [7, 8]

a = [1, 2, 3]
b = [1, 2, 3]
foo(a, b)
print(a, b) # [99, 2, 3] [1, 2, 3]
```

As a general style rule, functions should return a value but not mutate their arguments, while methods may mutate their arguments. For example, the following are built in:

- *obj*.sort() is a method that sorts the object *obj* and returns None, while

- sorted(*obj*) is a function that leaves *obj* unchanged but returns a sorted copy.

3.7 SHALLOW AND DEEP COPIES

Objects can contain references to other objects. If we copy the object, we normally get a ***shallow copy***: the references in the object are copied, but not the referenced objects themselves.

```
grades = [["Mary", "A+"], ["Don", "C-"]]
grades2 = grades[:]
grades2[0] = ["Bob", "B"]
grades2[1][1] = "F"
print(grades) # [['Mary', 'A+'], ['Don', 'F']]
print(grades2) # [['Bob', 'B'], ['Don', 'F']]
```

Here's what happened:

- grades is a list of two references, one to the list ["Mary", "A+"], and one to the list ["Don", "C-"].

- The assignment to grades2 makes a new list containing copies of those references.

- The assignment to grades2[0] changes the first reference in grades2 to a new list, ["Bob", "B"].

- grades2[1] is still a copy of the *reference* in grades[1], and both refer to the same list ["Don", "C-"], so the assignment to grades[1][1] changes the contents of that list.

Python provides a deepcopy method to make a completely independent *deep copy* of an object, to any level. This works even for cyclic objects, that is, objects that contain themselves.

```
import copy
grades3 = copy.deepcopy(grades)
grades3[1][1] = "D+"
# grades is unchanged
```

CHAPTER 4

Getting Fancy

4.1 STATEMENTS

This section describes Python statements that have not been previously covered, or that have more options than have previously been covered.

- import

  - import *module* — makes the named *module* available, after which an object or method named *name* in that module may be accessed by *module.name*. This prevents problems when the same name is imported from more than one module.

  - from *module* import *names* — imports the given names, which do not need to be prefixed by *module* and a dot.

  - from *module* import * — imports all names from *module*. Use with caution, as it may import names you are not even aware of.

  - import *module* as *modname* — makes the named *module* available, but instead of *module.name* you would use *modname.name*.

DOI: 10.1201/9781003356219-4

- from **module** import **name1** as **name2** — imports **name1** but renames it to **name2**.

- assert **expression1**, **expression2**

  - Does nothing if **expression1** is true, but raises an AssertError if **expression1** is false. The optional **expression2** is used as a message by the AssertError.

  - The assert statement is best thought of as "executable documentation." It can be used at the beginning of a function to express what is required of the parameters, or in the middle or at the end to claim something about what has just been computed. It can also be used as a built-in test case.

- **var1**, ... , **varN** = **expr1**, ... , **exprN**

  - Simultaneous assignment. The variables on the left are assigned the values of the expressions on the right. There must be exactly as many variables as expressions. This is just a special case of tuple packing and unpacking.

  - a, b = b, a is a particularly simple way to swap the values of a and b.

- break

  - If break is executed within a while or for loop, it causes the loop to exit.

  - If break is executed within nested loops, only the innermost loop is exited.

  - If the loop exits because of a break, a following else clause will not be executed. (Possibly unique to Python, loops may have an else clause.)

- continue

  - If continue is executed within a while or for loop, any remaining statements within the loop are skipped over, and control returns to the top of the loop (to the test in a while loop, or the next value in a for loop).

  - continue within nested loops applies to the innermost loop.

- del *variable*

  - Causes the variable to cease to exist (become unbound).

- else:

  - Both a while loop and a for loop may be followed by an else clause. The code in the else clause is executed when the loop exits normally, but is not executed if the loop terminates as the result of a break or a return.

- exec(*arg*)

  - Executes a string, a file that has been opened, or a code object *arg*. Code objects are not covered in this book.

  - exec is actually a function, but it returns None as its value, so it is often used as if it were a statement.

  - exec is **not secure**, so do not use it if there is any chance that the *arg* contains malicious or harmful code.

- nonlocal *variables*

  - Functions may be nested inside other functions. By default, an inner function can access but not change the variables of an enclosing function. If the inner function declares variables to be nonlocal, it can both access them and change them.

  - The rules are very similar to those of local and global variables.

- pass

  - The pass statement does nothing. It is occasionally useful when the syntax requires the presence of a statement, but there is nothing in particular to be done.

  - An ellipsis (three dots, ...) is the same as pass.

- print(*expr1*, ... , *exprN*, sep=*sepString*, end=*endString*, file=*outputFile*)

  - Evaluates and prints the expressions, with *sepString* between them, and *endString* after the last expression, on *outputFile*. The keyword arguments sep, end, and file may be omitted, with the default values ' ' (a single space), '\n' (a newline), and stdout, respectively.

- raise

  - raise *Exception* raises the named *Exception*, which might be handled later by a try-except statement. Python provides a large number of exception types, or you can define your own by subclassing Exception.

  - raise *Exception*(*expression*) raises the named *Exception*, and uses the result of the expression as a message in the exception.

  - raise by itself in an except clause re-raises the same exception.

4.2 IDENTIFIERS

Identifiers begin with a letter or underscore and may contain letters, underscores, and digits; case is significant. Unicode characters may be used.

By convention, class names begin with a capital letter. Other names do not.

In a class, you often want **private** instance variables—that is, fields that cannot be accessed or altered except from within the class. There is no way to do this in Python. Instead, some programmers have adopted the convention of putting an underscore as the first character in the name of a variable that they wish to be private, or two underscores if they really, really wish it were private. This is the programming version of putting a note on your front door that says, "Please don't burgle my house."

A variable name may consist of a single underscore. This name is often used when a variable is required but not actually used for anything.

```
for _ in range(0, 3):
    print("Hello!")
```

Built-in "dunder" names begin and end with two underscores. You should not name your own variables and methods this way.

4.3 TYPE HINTS

Python is a **dynamically typed** language. That is, the type of a variable name is the type of whatever value it holds at the moment.

Beginning with Python 3.5, you can enter **type hints** to specify what type of value a variable is expected to hold. These hints are treated as comments; they have absolutely no effect on the running program. Some IDEs can use type hints to do some static code checking, and this may become more prevalent in the future.

The following example demonstrates the syntax for hinting the types of variables, parameters, and function return values.

```
def indent(line: str, amount: int) -> str:
    indented_line:str = ' ' * amount + line
    return indented_line
```

To construct more complex type hints, import the typing module.

```
from typing import List, Set, Dict, Union, Optional
```

With this import, you can use type hints such as List[int], Set [int], Dict[str, str], Union[int, float], and Optional[str], as well as more complex type hints such as List[Set[int]]. The Union type hint specifies that the value may be any of the listed types, while the Optional type hint specifies that the value is either the given type or None.

A type hint may be assigned a name, after which the name can be used as a type hint. This can be very helpful for documenting complex data structures.

```
Number = Union[int, float]
```

4.4 NUMBERS

A **decimal integer** consists of either the number 0, or a sequence of digits not beginning with 0.

A **binary integer** consists of binary digits (0, 1), beginning with 0b or 0B.

An **octal integer** consists of a sequence of octal digits (0 to 7), beginning with 0o or 0O.

A **hexadecimal integer** consists of a sequence of hex digits (0 to 9 and a to f or A to F), beginning with 0x or 0X.

A **floating point** ("real") number includes a decimal point, an exponent suffix, or both. The exponent consists of the letter e or E, an optional sign, and one or more digits, for example, 1.7e-12.

An *imaginary number* consists of a decimal integer or a floating point number, suffixed by j (*not* i) or J.

A *complex number* consists of the sum or difference of an integer or floating-point number and an imaginary number.

To convert a string to a number, use the functions int(s), float(s), and complex(s). A ValueError will result if the string is malformed; in particular, a string representing a complex number cannot contain any spaces: 3+5j is okay, but 3 + 5j is not).

To convert a number to a string, use str(x) for a decimal representation, or bin(i), oct(i), or hex(i) for a string representation of the integer i as binary, octal, or hexadecimal, respectively.

To convert a number to or from a Unicode character, use the functions chr(n) or ord(c), respectively.

4.5 STRINGS

A *string* is written as a sequence of zero or more characters enclosed in single quotes ('...'), double quotes ("..."), triple single quotes ('''...'''), or triple double quotes ("""..."""). It can be treated as a list of characters.

Triply-quoted strings may extend across several lines, and include the line breaks as part of the string, unless the line break is immediately preceded by a backslash (\).

A *raw string* is a string prefixed with r or R. In a raw string the backslash does not escape characters; all characters stand for themselves. This is especially useful when writing regular expressions.

Regular expressions in Python follow the POSIX standards, and are usually written as raw strings. They will not be covered here.

The function eval(***string***) evaluates ***string*** as a Python expression and returns the result. If you use this, be sure ***string*** does not contain malicious code.

4.6 F-STRINGS

There are three ways of formatting a string: Using ***f-strings***, using the format method, and using the old-style % formatting. Generally the f-string method is recommended.

A formatted string, or ***f-string***, is prefixed with f or F. In an f-string, *any expression* surrounded by braces, {}, is replaced by its value.

- print(f'Area is {5*7/2}.')
  - Prints: Area is 17.5.

In Python 3.8 and later, if an expression in braces ends with an equals sign, the expression as well as the result is printed.

- print(f'Area is {5*7/2=}.')
  - Prints: Area is 5*7/2=17.5.

If you actually want to print braces inside an f-string, escaping them with a backslash does not work. Instead, double them ('{{' or '}}').

Formatting codes can be used. For example, the format :9.3f means to display a floating point number in 9 total spaces, with 3 digits after the decimal point.

- print(f'Area is {5*7/2:9.3f}.')
  - Prints: Area is   17.500.

The syntax of the formatting codes is quite complex, and will not be covered here. Instead, we will just give a few simple examples.

```
f'{"abc":6}'   is  'abc   '
f'{"abc":>6}'  is  '   abc'
f'{123:6d}'    is  '   123'
f'{123:<6d}'   is  '123   '
f'{pi:6.2f}'   is  '3.14'
f'{pi:<6.2f}'  is  '3.14  '
```

The syntax of the format method is *string*.format(*values*). As with an f-string, the string contains braces, but the braces contain formatting codes, not expressions. For example:

```
print('pi is {:8.4f}'.format(pi))
```

This code will print the string 'pi is   3.1416', with three spaces between the word is and the 3.

Besides formatting codes, the braces in the string given to the format method may contain simple integers. Each integer is taken as an index into the list of *values*. So, for example,' {1} {0} {1}'.format(1, 2) returns the string '2 1 2'.

The old-style % formatting uses the % percent sign both within the string to denote substitution locations and after the string as an operator. For example,'%s = %i' % ('x', 7) results in the string 'x = 7'. This formatting style is no longer recommended and will not be discussed further here.

4.7 BIT OPERATIONS

The following *bit operators* may be applied to integers.

- ~ bitwise complement
- & bitwise and

- | bitwise or

- ^   bitwise exclusive or

- <<   left shift (right operand is the amount to shift the left operand)

- \>\>   right shift (right operand is the amount to shift the left operand)

These operators work on the binary representation of integers; that is, each integer is represented as a binary number. The integer 0 consists of all zero bits, and -1 consists of all one bits.

- *Bitwise complement* changes every 1 to a 0 and every 0 to a 1. Numerically, the result is the same as changing the sign of the number, then subtracting 1.

- *Bitwise and* gives a 1 when the corresponding bits of both operands are 1, and 0 otherwise.

- *Bitwise or* gives a 1 when the corresponding bits of one or both operands are 1, and 0 otherwise.

- *Bitwise exclusive or* gives a 1 when the corresponding bits of the two operands are different, and 0 otherwise.

- *Left shift* moves all bits to the left, filling in with zeros.

- *Right shift* moves all bits to the right, with some disappearing off the left end, and zeros coming in on the right.

4.8 LIST COMPREHENSIONS

A *list comprehension* is a way of computing a list from a collection of values. The collection may be a list, a tuple, a set, the keys of a dictionary, a string, or anything that can be stepped through. A list comprehension may include optional if tests.

- [*expression* for *variable* in *collection*] is a new list formed by binding each value in the *collection* in turn to the *variable*, then evaluating the *expression*.

- [*expression* for *variable* in *collection* if *condition*] is a new list formed by binding each value in the *collection* in turn to the *variable*, then if the *condition* is satisfied with this binding, evaluating the *expression*.

List comprehensions are powerful and worth getting to know. Here are some simple uses:

- To apply an expression to every element of a list: [2 * x for x in [1, 2, 3]] returns [2, 4, 6].

- To remove unwanted elements from a list:
  [x for x in [1, 0, 2] if x > 0] returns [1, 2].

4.9 ITERATORS

An *iterable object* is any object that can be stepped through. Iterable objects include lists, sets, tuples, strings, dictionaries, ranges, and files. An *iterator* is an object that keeps track of where it is in stepping through an iterable object, and provides the next value as needed.

For example, you can get a *list iterator* by saying it = iter([2, 3, 5]). You can step through the elements of this list by repeatedly calling next(it); this will return 2, then 3, then 5. Yet another call to next(it) will raise a StopIteration exception.

This is exactly how a for loop works. It starts by getting an iterator for an iterable object such as a list or range. Then it uses the iterator to get a single value from the object, executes the loop body, then returns to the iterator to get the next value. The for loop exits when it gets a StopIteration exception.

You can make your own objects iterable. To do this:

- The iterable class must contain an __iter__ method to create and return a new iterator object, in a state where all items are yet to be delivered.

- The iterator class contains at least two methods:

  - an __init__ method which takes the iterable as a parameter, saves it in an instance variable, and does whatever other setup is necessary;

  - a __next__ method to find or compute the next value. It should raise a StopIteration exception if called when there are no more values to be returned.

- These classes can be combined, so that the iterable object is its own iterator. In this case, the class contains a __next__ method, and the __iter__ method just returns self.

As a simple example, we can write an iterable class MyList which holds a list, and an iterator class Reverser which will iterate through the list in reverse order.

```python
class MyList():
    def __init__(self, ls):
        self.ls = ls

    def __iter__(self):
        return Reverser(self.ls)

class Reverser():
    def __init__(self, ls):
        self.ls = ls
        self.index = len(self.ls)

    def __next__(self):
        self.index = self.index - 1
```

```
    if self.index >= 0:
        return self.ls[self.index]
    raise StopIteration
```

The iterator's job is to keep track of where it is in the iteration, using its own variables and not those of the iterable object. The iterator shouldn't affect or modify the iterable object. This rule allows two or more iterators to run simultaneously on the same object without interfering with each other.

If the classes are combined so that the iterable is its own iterator, then only one iterator at a time can be supported.

A for loop may use any iterable object. In for loops, the StopIteration exception does not result in an error; it merely terminates the for loop. For example,

```
ls = MyList([1, 2, 3, 4])
for e in ls:
    print(e)
```

Alternatively, you can use the iter and next methods directly, and handle the StopIteration exception yourself. This is essentially what the previous for loop is doing.

```
ls = MyList([1, 2, 3, 4])
it = iter(ls)
while True:
    try:
        print(next(it))
    except StopIteration:
        break
```

An iterator can be used only once; when it raises the StopIteration exception, it's done, and cannot be reset. Instead of resetting an iterator, you can simply create another one.

If you have an iterator it that returns a *finite* number of values and you need a list of those values, just say list(it).

4.10 GENERATORS

A **generator** is a kind of iterator. It generates values one at a time, as needed, but it isn't necessarily tied to a particular kind of object.

One kind of **generator expression** looks just like a list comprehension, except that the enclosing brackets are replaced by parentheses. Generators may be used wherever an iterator may be used, such as in a for loop. Example:

```
word = 'generator'
gen = (c for c in word if c in 'aeiou')

for i in gen:
    print(i, end=' ')
```

This code will print e e a o.

> **Caution:** A generator is a kind of iterator, so after it returns all its values, it is "used up." If the above for loop were called a second time, it would not print anything, because the variable gen would hold an empty generator.

You can write functions that act as generators, by using yield instead of return. Here is an example generator for powers of 2:

```
def powers_of_two():
    n = 2
    for i in range(0, 5):
        yield n
        n *= 2
```

When this function is called, it returns a *generator*, not a number. You can use this generator in a for loop, the same way g was used above, and you will get the values 2, 4, 8, 16, and 32.

```
gen = powers_of_two()
for n in gen:
    print(n)
```

Since e is an iterator, you can use next(gen) to get the next value. In this case you will have to handle the exception yourself.

```
gen = powers_of_two()
while True:
    try:
        print(next(gen))
    except StopIteration:
        break
```

Here's how this works:

- The call gen = powers_of_two() returns a generator and puts it in gen.

- The first call of next(gen) executes the generator down to the yield statement, and returns the yielded value, just like a normal return statement. But in addition, the generator remembers where it left off.

- A subsequent call to next(gen) will cause the generator to resume execution where it left off, that is, immediately after the yield statement. All the values of local variables will have been retained. As far as the generator is concerned, it is as if the yield had never happened. In this example, the for loop keeps running.

- You can have multiple yield statements in a generator. The function will remember at which yield it left off, and will continue from there.

- Just as with iterators, a generator will raise a StopIteration exception when there are no more values to return. This happens automatically when it reaches the end of the function, or if it reaches a return statement.

4.11 PARAMETERS AND ARGUMENTS

With no additional syntax, **arguments** (expressions in a function call) are matched to **parameters** (variables in a function definition) by position. The first parameter gets the value of the first expression, and so on.

Parameters in a function definition may be:

- A simple variable name, matched and bound to an argument by position. Positional parameters must precede any other parameters.

- **variable=value**, to give a default value for missing arguments.

- ***args**, to accept multiple arguments as a single tuple. By convention, the name args is usually used for this purpose.

- ****kwargs**, to accept multiple keyword arguments as a dictionary. By convention, the name kwargs (keyword arguments) is usually used for this purpose.

*args or ****kwargs** can only be used as the last parameter, as either one collects all remaining arguments.

Arguments in a function call may be:

- An expression.

- **name=value**, to give a value to the parameter with that name. This is called a **named argument** or **keyword argument**.

If both positional and keyword arguments are used, all positional arguments must precede keyword arguments.

- *iterable*, to pass the values of an iterable as separate arguments.

- **dictionary*, to pass in values to multiple parameters by name.

Starting with Python 3.8, arguments can be forced to be positional only. A single slash, /, in place of a parameter means that all earlier arguments must be positional. An asterisk, *, in place of a parameter means that all arguments after that must be keyword. For example, given the function

```
def foo(a, b, /, c, d, *, e, f):
    print(a, b, c, d, e, f)
```

Arguments for a and b must be by position only; arguments for e and f must be keyword arguments. Arguments for c and d may be either (but since positional arguments must precede keyword arguments, d cannot be positional if c is keyword).

Many of the functions described in the official Python documentation appear to have a single asterisk as a parameter, for example, os.remove(path, *, dir_fd=None). This is a documentation convention to indicate that the subsequent arguments can only be given as named arguments. It does *not* mean you should put an asterisk in the function call.

4.12 FUNCTIONAL PROGRAMMING

Definitions of *functional programming* differ, but in general include the following:

- Functions are objects, and can be treated like any other value.

- Variables are *single-assignment*; once given a value, they are never changed.

- All functions are *pure*; the value returned by a function depends only on the arguments given to it, and if called again with the same arguments, it will produce the same value. This excludes any use of global variables or other external factors, such as the system clock.

Functional programming is widely regarded as an ivory-tower technique, not suitable for day-to-day programming. This is not the place to challenge that viewpoint, other than to note that all modern programming languages support functional programming to some extent.

In this book we consider only the first point above: that functions are objects. We will consider only a single example of such a use.

The following function will find the largest value in a nonempty list of values:

```python
def biggest(values):
    big = values[0]
    for v in values:
        if v > big:
            big = v
    return big
```

Since > can also be used to compare strings, this function can be used to find the lexicographically largest string in a list of strings. But for almost any other purpose (finding the smallest number, the longest string, etc.) you have to write another, almost identical function.

Instead of writing more and more functions, we can replace the > with a generic test:

```
def most(values, more):
    best = values[0]
    for v in values:
        if more(v, best):
            best = v
    return best

def larger(a, b):
    return a > b
```

And we can call the most function like this:

```
most([1, 6, 1, 8, 0], larger)
```

or like this:

```
def longer(a, b):
    return len(a) > len(b)

most(["a", "generic", "list"], longer)
```

This still results in a lot of little functions such as larger and longer. Python also provides *literal functions*, sometimes called *anonymous functions* because they have no name. Literal functions are intended to be used only in the one place that they are written. For historical reasons, a literal function is introduced by the keyword lambda. For example,

```
lambda a, b: len(a) > len(b)
```

and it can be used like this:

```
print(most(["a", "generic", "list"],
    lambda a, b: len(a) > len(b)))
```

A lambda expression consists of the keyword lambda, any number of parameters, a colon, and a single expression. In this example the result of the expression is a boolean, but it could be of any type.

Python has a number of built-in functions that take a function as a parameter. Here are some of the most generally useful:

- map(*function*, *iterable*) returns an iterator whose next function will get the next value of the *iterable*, apply the *function* to it, and return the result.

- filter(*predicate*, *iterable*) returns an iterator whose next function will return the next value of the *iterable* that satisfies the *predicate*.

- functools.reduce(*binaryFunction*,   *iterable*)   applies *binaryFunction* to the first two elements of the *iterable*. It then repeatedly applies *binaryFunction* to the current result and the next member of *iterable*, returning a single value as the result. (**Note:** reduce must be imported from functools.)

Examples: If my_list is [3, 1, 4, 1, 6], then

- map(lambda x: x * x, my_list) will return the values 9, 1,16, 1, 36.

- filter(lambda x: x > 1, my_list) will return the values 3, 4, 6.

- reduce(lambda x, y: x + y, my_list) will return 15.

CHAPTER 5

Testing

C ODE HAS TO BE TESTED. It is unusual for any significant piece of code to run correctly the first time.

One all-too-common approach is to try out the code as it is being written, conclude that everything is correct, and do nothing to preserve the tests. This does nothing to future-proof the code against more subtle errors, and makes it more difficult to modify the code as requirements change.

A **test framework** is software that:

1. allows tests to be written in a simple, standardized form; and

2. allows the tests to be run with an absolute minimum of effort.

In the following sections we will discuss two frameworks, doctest and unittest.

DOI: 10.1201/9781003356219-5

5.1 PHILOSOPHY

Use of a proper test framework has a large number of advantages:

- Code is much more likely to be correct.

- Code typically takes less time to produce, because debugging time is reduced.

- Functions written to be tested tend to be much smaller and single purpose.

- Functions written to be tested provide a clean separation between computation and I/O.

- The existence of a *test suite* (a collection of tests) makes it easier and safer to modify the code at some later date.

A good test framework gives the programmer the ability to run the tests quickly, usually with a single button click, and see with a single glance if there are any errors. Any tests that require more than this will not be run frequently, if at all, thus negating the value of having them.

To write testable code,

- Write many small functions that each do one thing, rather than a few large functions that do a lot of things.

- Write the tests as you go. Many authorities recommend writing the tests before writing the code to be tested; this helps clarify what the code is supposed to do, and also helps the programmer see the interface from the users point of view.

  - It can be difficult or impossible to write tests for pre-existing or legacy code.

- Minimize the use of global variables, and avoid them entirely if you can. Functions whose values depend only on their arguments are much easier to test in isolation.

- Strictly separate functions that do computation from functions that do input or output, and test only the former.

  - Functions that do I/O involve the programmer, so they prevent the use of single-click testing. While there are techniques for testing these functions, those are advanced techniques not covered here.

5.2 DOCTEST

A lot of testing is done on an ad hoc basis—the programmer types in function calls at the Python prompt (>>>), and looks to see if the result is correct. Doctest provides a very low-effort way to preserve these tests.

To use doctest, simply copy the ad hoc tests done at the prompt, including the >>> prompt, and paste them into the doc comment for the function being tested. The following get_digits function returns a list of all the digits in an integer or a string:

```
def get_digits(number):
    """Return a list of digits in an int or string."""
    string = str(number)
    return [x for x in string if x.isdigit()]
```

Then the programmer might run some tests:

```
>>> get_digits("124c41")
['1', '2', '4', '4', '1']
>>> get_digits(1213141)
['1', '2', '1', '3', '1', '4', '1']
```

To use doctest, the ad hoc tests done at the Python prompt are copied and pasted into the docstring.

```python
def get_digits(number):
    """Return a list of digits in an int or string."""
    >>> get_digits("124c41")
    ['1', '2', '4', '4', '1']
    >>> get_digits(1213141)
    ['1', '2', '1', '3', '1', '4', '1']
    """
    string = str(number)
    return [x for x in string if x.isdigit()]
```

To run these tests again, use:

```python
import doctest
doctest.testmod()
```

The testmod method will locate all the ad hoc tests in the comments and run them again. It will print information about all failed tests; if all tests pass, testmod doesn't print anything (though it does return a summary result).

Notes:

- Exceptions raised by a test can be tested just like any other result, by copying the printed result into the docstring.

- The >>> prompt may begin in any column, but the output must begin in the same column.

- For code that extends over multiple lines, the ... continuation prompt should also be copied into the docstring.

- Tabs in the output will be converted to spaces, causing the doctest to fail.

- A blank line in the output is taken as the end of the output.

Tests may be put in a separate file and executed with the doctest.testfile(*path*) method.

While doctest is a least-effort way to preserve some tests, it isn't as flexible as unit testing.

5.3 UNIT TESTING

A **unit test** is a test of the methods in a single class. A **test case** tests the response of a single method to a particular set of inputs. To do unit testing,

- import unittest

- import *fileToBeTested*   or
  from *fileToBeTested* import *

  - **Reminder:** If you use from file import * then you don't have to precede every function call with the name of the file it was imported from.

- Write a class *SomeName*(unittest.TestCase). Within the class,

  - Define methods setUp(self) and tearDown(self), if wanted. These are both optional.

  - Provide one or more test*Something*(self) methods. You may include other methods, but the names of test methods must begin with test.

- At the end of the test file, put unittest.main().

Here's what unittest.main() does. For each and every method whose name begins with test, the unittest.main method calls setUp() if you have provided one, then calls the test method, then calls tearDown() if you have provided one. So, every test is sandwiched between setUp and tearDown.

The purpose of the setUp method is to make sure everything is in a known, pristine state before calling the test method. In this way you can make sure that the results of running one test do not affect the results of a later test.

The purpose of tearDown is to remove artifacts (such as files) that may have been created. It is used much less frequently than setUp.

Each test method should typically test only one function, though it may call that function many times. If a function behaves differently for different kinds of input (for example, positive or negative numbers), it's a good idea to write multiple test methods.

Here is a trivial example of a test method:

```
def test_add(self):
    self.assertEqual(4, add(2, 2))
    self.assertEqual(0, add(2, -2))
```

It is conventional to put the expected result (4 or 0) first, and the function call (add) last.

If any assertion in a test method fails, the test fails and the remaining assertions in that method are not tested. For this reason, test methods should not become too long.

If the method to be tested is in a class C, and you used import C rather than from C import *, you must also use the class name, for example, self.assertEqual(4, C.add(2, 2)).

Here are the most commonly used assertion methods:

- self.assertEqual(*expected*, *actual*)

- self.assertAlmostEqual(*expected*, *actual*) for floating point numbers.

- self.assertTrue(*boolean*) and self.assertFalse (*boolean*).

More assertion methods are given in Appendix F.

You can test whether a function raises an exception when it is supposed to, but this test has a special form. This is necessary because arguments to a function are evaluated before the function is called. For example, if you said

```
self.assertRaises(ZeroDivisionError, 5/0)
```

then the argument 5/0 would be evaluated and would raise the exception *before* assertRaises can be called.

The solution is to pass the function name in separately from its arguments:

```
self.assertRaises(exception, function_name, arguments)
```

This allows the assertRaises function to call the function to be tested within a try-except block, and handle it appropriately.

When testing is not being done, a common idiom is to put a call to the main function as the last line in the code file, for example, main(). This causes the main method to run immediately after the file is loaded. When doing unit testing, this is undesirable. Instead, replace that line with

```
if __name__ == '__main__':
    main()
```

and put the following code at the end of the test file:

```
unittest.main()
```

In this way, the program will be run if loaded from the program file, and the tests will be run if loaded from the test file.

5.4 UNIT TEST EXAMPLE

In file get_digits.py:

```python
def get_digits(number):
    """Return a list of digits in an int or string."""
    string = str(number)
    return [x for x in string if x.isdigit()]

def main():
    s = input("Enter something: ")
    digits = get_digits(s)
    print("Digits found:", digits)
    if digits != []:
        main()

# Call main() if and only if started from this file
if __name__ == '__main__':
    main()
```

In file get_digits_test.py:

```python
import unittest
from get_digits import *

class test_get_digits(unittest.TestCase):

    def test_get_digits(self):
        s = get_digits("<0.12-34 56abc789x")
        self.assertEqual(list("0123456789"),
                            get_digits(s))
        self.assertEqual(list("1230"),
                            get_digits(1230))
unittest.main()
```

5.5 TEST SUITES

Unit tests can be combined into a *test suite*. If the file test-foo.py contains the class TestFoo, and the file testbar.py contains the class TestBar, the test suite can be written like this:

```
import unittest
import testfoo, testbar

def suite():
    suite = unittest.TestSuite()
    suite.addTest(
        unittest.makeSuite(
            testfoo.TestFoo))
    suite.addTest(
        unittest.makeSuite(
            testbar.TestBar))
    return suite

if __name__ == '__main__':
    test_suite = suite()
    runner = unittest.TextTestRunner()
    runner.run (test_suite)
```

CHAPTER 6

Graphical User Interfaces

6.1 DIALOGS

There are several GUI (Graphical User Interface, pronounced "gooey") systems that can be used with Python. This chapter discusses Tkinter, which comes bundled with the standard Python distribution.

Many programs do not require a full GUI, just a dialog box or two. Tkinter provides a number of these. To use them, import `messagebox`, `simpledialog`, and/or `filedialog` from `tkinter`.

- `messagebox.showinfo(`***title, message***`)`

- `messagebox.showwarning(`***title, message***`)`

- `messagebox.showerror(`***title, message***`)`

  - All the above are essentially the same; the difference is which icon is displayed. All provide for a ***title***, a ***message***, and an `OK` button.

DOI: 10.1201/9781003356219-6

- *result* = messagebox.askyesno(*title*, *question*)

  - This provides No and Yes buttons, which return False or True, respectively.

- *result* = simpledialog.askfloat(*title*, *message*)

- *result* = simpledialog.askinteger(*title*, *message*)

- *result* = simpledialog.askstring(*title*, *message*)

  - Allows the user to enter a floating point number, integer, or string. Provides Cancel and OK buttons; if the dialog is canceled, the value returned is None.

- *input_file* = filedialog.askopenfilename(initialdir= *path*, title=*title*)

  - Asks for a file to be read in. If an initialdir argument is provided, navigation starts from that point.

- *output_file* = filedialog.asksaveasfilename(initialdir= *path*)

  - Asks for a location in which to save a file. If an initialdir argument is provided, navigation starts from that point.

6.2 TKINTER

GUI programs work differently than programs without a GUI. Instead of all code under control of a main method, the program creates a GUI, and thereafter everything that happens is a result of some user interaction with the GUI. For example, the user clicks a button, and that causes certain code to be executed.

Start with

```
from tkinter import *
import tkinter.ttk
```

After that, your code should create a "root" window,

```
top = Tk()
```

Next, populate the window with widgets (see below).

Finally, turn over execution to the GUI:

```
top.mainloop()
```

There are three main tasks to be performed:

1. Create some widgets (buttons, text areas, etc.).

2. Arrange the widgets in the window.

3. Associate code with some of the widgets.

You can execute some initialization code before calling `mainloop`, but once you call `mainloop`, the GUI is in control.

A minor annoyance is that whenever Tkinter is used to build a GUI, it must display a "root window." This is a small window that appears on your screen and has no function. To eliminate it, create a root window yourself and immediately hide it. This only needs to be done once.

```
import tkinter
root = tkinter.Tk()
root.withdraw()
```

6.3 CREATING WIDGETS

The window that opens when you run a GUI program is a *container*: it can contain *widgets* (buttons, text areas, etc.). A *frame* is a container that you can put inside a window, or in another frame.

There are 15 types of widgets in Tkinter, each with many options, indicated with option=*value*. This will cover only the most common types and options. In the following, we assume that the window is called top.

- *fr* = Frame(*parent, option, ...*)

  - This is a container for widgets. The parent may be the top-level window (top) or another Frame. Some useful options are bg=*color*, the background color (as a color name or hex number) and bd=*n*, the border width in pixels.

- *but* = Button(*parent*, text=*string*, command=*function_name*)

  - Creates a button containing the string, which when clicked will call the named function. Parameters cannot be supplied to the function.

- *lab* = Label(*parent*, text=*string*)

  - Creates a label that can be displayed but not edited by the user.

  - To change the text, use *lab*.configure(text=*new_text*).

- *ent* = Entry(*parent*, width=*n*)

  - Creates a rectangle large enough to display approximately *n* characters, into which the user can type a single line of text. More than *n* characters may be entered, but they may not all be visible.

  - To retrieve the text, call *ent*.get().

- *txt* = Text(*parent*, width=*num_characters*, height=*num_lines*)

  - Creates a rectangle *num_characters* wide and *num_lines* high, into which the user can type multiple lines of text.

Any number of lines may be entered, but only the specified number will be visible.

- To retrieve the text, call *txt*.get(1.0, END).

- To delete all text, use *txt*.delete(1.0, END).

- To insert text, use *txt*.insert(END, text).

- *var* = IntVar()

  - Defines *var* as an IntVar(see Checkbutton below).

- *chk* = Checkbutton(*parent*, text=*string*, variable=*var*, command=*function*)

  - The *var* must have been defined with IntVar().

  - Creates a checkbox with the given text.

  - *var*.get() will return 1 if checked, 0 if not checked.

6.4 PUTTING WIDGETS INTO THE GUI

There are three methods for arranging widgets into the main window and into frames: pack, grid, and place. Only one of these methods should be used in any given window or frame.

Complex layouts can be created by putting multiple frames into the window and/or into other frames, and using different layouts for the window and for each frame.

widget.pack(*options*) just adds the widget to the window or frame. Options are:

- side=*side* where *side* is one of LEFT, RIGHT, TOP, or BOTTOM to add widgets starting from that side.

- expand=True to expand the widget to fill available space.

- fill=*how* to expand the widget, where *how* is X (horizontally), Y (vertically), BOTH, or NONE.

widget.grid(*options*) adds the widget into a grid (two-dimensional table). Options are:

- row=*n* The row to put the widget in. Default is the first available row.

- column=*n* The column to put the widget in; default is 0.

- rowspan=*n* The number of rows the widget should occupy.

- columnspan=*n* The number of columns the widget should occupy.

- ipadx=*n*, ipady=*n* The amount (in pixels) to pad the widget, horizontally and vertically.

- sticky=*d* Where to put the widget if in a larger space. *d* is one of N, S, E, W, NE, SE, NW, SW.

widget.place(*options*) specifies exactly where to place each widget. Options are:

- x=*pixels*, y=*pixels* The x and y position of the anchor point of the widget, relative to the parent.

- anchor=*d* Which part of the widget the x and y refer to, where d is one of N, S, E, W, NE, SE, NW, SW. The default is NW (top-left corner).

- bordermode=OUTSIDE to take the parent's border into account when positioning the widget, else INSIDE (INSIDE is the default).

- height=*pixels*, width=*pixels* The height and width of the widget, in pixels.

- relx=*float*, rely=*float* The x and y position, as a fraction between 0.0 and 1.0, of the width and height of the parent.

- relwidth=*float*, relheight=*float* The size of the widget, as a fraction between 0.0 and 1.0, of the width and height of the parent.

6.5 TKINTER EXAMPLE

Here is a program for rolling a single die. When executed, the window should appear at the top-left corner of your screen. Exit the program by closing the window.

```
from tkinter import *
import tkinter.ttk
from random import randint

def roll():
    n = str(randint(1, 6))
    result.configure(text=n)

top = Tk()

roll_button = Button(top, text='Roll', command=roll)
result = Label(top, width=12)

roll_button.grid(row=0)
result.grid(row=1)
```

Afterword

T HIS LITTLE VOLUME HAS covered the basics of Python 3. Unlike many Python books, it has also introduced functional programming, unit testing, and GUI implementation with Tkinter.

Python has a large number of library routines to explore. As with any language, there are plenty of surprises in odd corners in both the syntax and semantics.

Beyond this, there are a large number of Python packages readily available—NumPy for scientific applications, NLTK for natural language processing, and SciPy for machine learning, to name a few of the most popular.

If you have made it this far in this book, *and* have tried out things as you went, you should have a solid foundation for learning more, and going wherever your interests and requirements take you.

Happy programming!

Appendix A:
String Methods

HERE ARE SOME OF THE string methods available from the string module (in alphabetical order):

- *string*.center(*int*) returns a copy of *string* centered in a string of length *int*.

- *string*.count(*substring*) returns the number of non-overlapping occurrences of *substring* in *string*.

- *string*.endswith(*suffix*) returns True if string ends with *suffix*.

- *string*.find(*substring*) returns the index of the beginning of the first occurrence of *substring* in *string*, or -1 if not found.

- *string*.format(*values*) returns a string with the values inserted into placeholders of the form {*index*} or {*variable*}. Placeholders may contain an optional :*formatting_code*.

- *string*.isalnum() tests whether all characters are alphanumeric (letters or digits).

- *string*. isalpha() tests whether all characters are alphabetic.

- *string*. isdigit() tests whether all characters are digits.

- *string*. isidentifier() tests whether *string* is a nonempty string consisting of letters, digits, and/or underscores, and does not begin with a digit.

- *string*. islower() tests whether all letters in *string* are lowercase—False if the string contains no letters.

- *string*. isprintable() tests whether the string does not contain control characters.

- *string*. isspace() tests whether all characters are whitespace (spaces, tabs, newlines, some Unicode characters)—False if *string* is the empty string.

- *string*. isupper() tests whether all letters in *string* are uppercase—False if the string contains no letters.

- *string*. join(*list_of_strings*) returns a single string, with the elements of the *list_of_strings* separated by *string*.

- *string*. ljust(*int*) returns a copy of *string* left-justified in a field of length *int*.

- *string*. lower() returns a copy of *string* with all letters lowercased.

- *string1*. partition(*string2*) returns a 3-tuple: (the part of *string1* before *string2*, *string2* itself, the part after *string2*).

- *string1*. replace(*string2*, *string3*) returns a copy of *string1* with all occurrences of *string2* replaced by *string3*.

- *string*. rjust(*int*) returns a copy of the string right-justified in a field of length *int*.

- *string1*.split(*string2*) returns a list of the substrings of *string1* that are separated by *string2*. If *string2* is omitted, whitespace is used as the separator.

- *string*.splitlines() returns a list of the lines in *string*, discarding newline characters.

- *string*.startswith(*prefix*) returns True if *string* starts with *prefix*.

- *string*.strip() returns a copy of *string* with all leading and trailing whitespace removed.

- *string*.upper() returns a copy of *string* with all letters uppercased.

In addition: A string may be treated as a list of characters, so all of the list methods can be applied to strings.

Appendix B:
Numerical Functions

Hᴇʀᴇ ᴀʀᴇ sᴏᴍᴇ ʙᴜɪʟᴛ-ɪɴ functions on numbers; you don't need to import these.

- abs(x) returns the absolute value of a number x (or the magnitude of a complex number).

- bin(int) returns a binary string representation of int.

- chr(int) returns the character whose Unicode representation is int. The inverse operation is ord.

- divmod(x, y) returns the tuple (x // y, x % y) for integers.

- float(x) converts a string or integer x to a floating point number.

- hex(int) returns a hexadecimal string representation of int.

- int(x) converts a string x to an integer, or truncates a float x to an integer.

- oct(int) returns an octal string representation of int.

- pow(*x, y*) returns *x* raised to the power *y*.

- round(*float*) returns the integer nearest to the given *float* value.

- round(*float, int*) returns *float* rounded to *int* digits after the decimal point.

The math module includes a lot of methods that are not available by default. Here are some of them.

- math.ceil(*x*) returns the smallest integer greater than or equal to *x*.

- math.floor(*x*) returns the largest integer smaller than or equal to *x*.

- math.trunc(*x*) returns the integer value obtained by dropping everything after the decimal point.

- math.gcd(*a, b*) returns the greatest common divisor of the two arguments.

- math.factorial(*n*) returns the product of the first *n* positive integers.

- math.comb(*n, k*) returns the number of possible subsets of size *k* from a set of *n* elements.

- math.perm(*n, k*) returns the number of possible ordered sequences of size *k*, where the elements are drawn without replacement from a set of *n* elements.

- math.sqrt(*x*) returns the square root of *x*.

- math.log(*x*), math.log2(*x*), math.log10(*x*), math.log (*x, b*) return the logarithm of *x* to the base *e*, 2, 10, or *b*, respectively.

- math.exp(*x*) returns e^x.

- The trignometric functions math.sin(x), math.cos(x), math.tan(x), math.asin(x), math.acos(x), and math.atan(x), where x is in radians.

- The hyperbolic functions math.sinh(x), math.cosh(x), math.tanh(x), math.asinh(x), math.acosh(x), and math.atanh(x), where x is in radians.

- The conversion functions math.degrees(*radians*) and math.radians(*degrees*).

- The math module also defines the constants math.pi, math.e, and math.tau.

Here are some of the functions that you get if you import the random module:

- random.choice(*seq*) returns an element chosen randomly from the sequence *seq*.

- random.shuffle(*seq*) shuffles the sequence *seq* in place (that is, the original list is changed).

- random.random() returns a random floating point number r in the range $0.0 \leq r < 1.0$.

- random.randint(*a, b*) returns a random integer r in the range $a \leq r \leq b$.

Reminder: If you import the functions individually or by using the from *module* import * version of the import statement, you can leave off the *module* prefix (in this case, math. and random.).

Appendix C:
Statistics

H ERE ARE SOME OF THE functions provided by the `statistics` module.

- `statistics.mean(`*`data`*`)` returns the mathematical "average" of the data, computed by adding the values and dividing their sum by the number of values.

- `statistics.median(`*`data`*`)` returns the "middle" number of the data, such that half the values are less than or equal to it, and half are greater than or equal to it. If there are an even number of values, the result is the mean of the two middle values.

- `statistics.mode(`*`data`*`)` returns the number that occurs most often in the data (or if a tie, the first such number).

For example,

```
from statistics import *
a = [1, 2, 3, 4, 5, 5, 78]
print(f"{mean(a)=}, {median(a)=}, {mode(a)=}")
```

prints:

```
mean(a)=14, median(a)=4, mode(a)=5
```

Here are some more functions:

- `statistics.stdev(`*data*`)` returns the sample standard deviation.

- `statistics.variance(`*data*`)` returns the sample variance.

Using the same value for a as above,

```
print(f"{stdev(a):6.2 f}, {variance(a):6.2 f}")
```

prints:

```
28.26, 798.67
```

The `statistics` module also includes functions for working with normal distributions.

Appendix D: Functions on Iterables

HERE ARE SOME FUNCTIONS that take iterable objects (lists, sets, tuples, strings, dictionaries, ranges, files, and possibly others).

- all(*iterable*) returns True if every element of *iterable* evaluates to a true value.

- any(*iterable*) returns True if at least one element of *iterable* evaluates to a true value.

- filter(*test*, *iterable*) returns an iterator for the items in *iterable* that pass the *test*.

- len(*iterable*) returns the number of elements in *iterable*.

- list(*iterable*) returns a list of the elements in *iterable*, in the same order.

- map(*function*, *iterable*) returns an iterator. Each value returned by the iterator will be the result of applying the *function* to the corresponding value of the *iterable*.

- max(*iterable*) returns the largest value in *iterable*.

- `min(`*iterable*`)` returns the smallest value in *iterable*.

- `set(`*iterable*`)` returns a set of the values in *iterable*.

- `sorted(`*iterable*`)` returns a list of the elements in *iterable*, in sorted order.

- `sum(`*iterable*`)` returns the sum of the values in *iterable*.

- `tuple(`*iterable*`)` returns a tuple of the elements in *iterable*, in the same order.

- `zip(`*iterable1*`,...,`*iterableN*`)` returns an iterator of *N*-tuples, where the first tuple contains the first value in each iterable, the second tuple contains the second value in each iterable, and so on. Iteration stops when any one of the iterables runs out of values.

- *element* `in` *iterable* returns `True` if *element* is in *iterable*.

- *element* `not in` *iterable* returns `True` if *element* is not in *iterable*.

Functions that take an iterable object can, in general, also take an iterator or a generator. If this is done, the iterator or generator will be passed in its current state, which may or may not be at the start of the iterable.

Some of the above functions have to examine every element of the iterable (`max`, for example). Others, like `any`, may or may not examine every element. Care should be taken not to call such a function with an iterator or generator that produces an infinite number of values.

Appendix E: Operating System Commands

Hᴇʀᴇ ᴀʀᴇ ᴀ ꜰᴇᴡ ᴏꜰ ᴛʜᴇ functions available when you import os:

- os.getcwd() gets the current working directory.

- os.chdir(*path*) changes the current working directory to *path*. Paths (given as strings) may be absolute or relative.

- os.listdir(path='.') returns a list containing the names of the entries in the directory '.'.

  - Note that path(not italicized) is a keyword, not a variable that can be replaced by some other name. In other functions, *path* (italicized) represents a variable containing a string, or the string itself.

- os.mkdir(*path*, mode=0o777, dir_fd=None) creates a directory named *path* with numeric mode 0o777.

- The mode is a Unix-style three-digit octal code. The three bits of each digit specify read, write, and execute permissions for owner, group, and world.

- os.remove(*path*, dir_fd=None) deletes the single file *path*; not for directories.

- os.rmdir(*path*, dir_fd=None) removes (deletes) the empty directory *path*.

- os.rename(*src*, *dst*) renames the file or directory *src* to *dst*.

- os.walk(*top*, topdown=True, onerror=None, followlinks=False) generates the file names in a directory tree by walking the tree either top-down or bottom-up. For each directory in the tree rooted at directory *top* (including *top* itself), it yields a 3-tuple (*dirpath*, *dirnames*, *filenames*).

Appendix F: Unit Test Methods

T HE FOLLOWING ARE SOME of the methods available in unittest, most of which are self-explanatory.

- assertEqual(*a*, *b*)

- assertNotEqual(*a*, *b*)

- assertAlmostEqual(*a*, *b*) # for floating point numbers

- assertAlmostEqual(*a*, *b*, *places*)

- assertTrue(*x*)

- assertFalse(*x*)

- assertIs(*a*, *b*) # tests for identity

- assertIsNot(*a*, *b*)

- assertIsNone(*x*)

- assertIsNotNone(*x*)

- assertIn(*a*, *b*)

- assertNotIn(*a*, *b*)

- assertIsInstance(*a*, *b*)

- assertNotInstance(*a*, *b*)

- assertRaises(*exception*, *function*, *arguments*)

All calls to these methods must be prefixed with self..

Each of these methods has an optional final parameter, which may be any expression. It is used as a message in the AssertionError to provide any necessary additional information.

These methods are not called directly. Instead, they should be put in one or more methods whose names begin with self.. Executing unittest.main() will find and execute all such methods.

Index

Printed in the United States
by Baker & Taylor Publisher Services